$6.00

anged by William Cummings, 1847

The Arkansas
Traveller

The Arkansas Traveller

Adapted for Today's Readers

by Liz Smith Parkhurst

illustrations by
Carron Bain Hocut

August House/Little Rock
PUBLISHERS

Special thanks are due to:

Carron Hocut, for bringing the text to life
Ira Hocut, for his impeccable production artwork
Jan Barger, for her artistic rendition of William Cummings'
"Arkansas Traveller" score
Ted Parkhurst, **Dee Brown**, **Shelley Cox**, and **Bill
McNeil**, for their invaluable and objective editorial assistance.

This book is dedicated to Ralph and Moppy Smith, with highest hopes that all parents will do for their children as these parents do for me:

They pray for good influences.

PREFACE:

THE CASE FOR NOT LETTING SLEEPING DOGS LIE

When I was eleven years old, if anyone would have asked me what "The Arkansas Traveller" was, I would have replied without a moment's hesitation that it was the name of the fifteen-foot used skiboat my brothers and I had just talked my father into purchasing. That boat, in conspiracy with a 40-horsepower Evinrude outboard motor (also used), faithfully pulled the Smith and Sadler children on water skis around Tomkin's Bend on Lake Ouachita for seven successive summers.

I cannot say with conviction that, during those years, any other definition of "The Arkansas Traveller" could have held more meaning for me than did those glorious mornings spent gliding over the blue-green waters, skiing double with either of my brothers,

and watching the world spin by from that unique perspective.

In 1975, the musical ensemble of Emerson, Lake and Palmer produced a brilliant piece — "Hoedown" — which was an electronic variation of the last movement of Aaron Copland's *Rodeo*. Other pieces of musical Americana had been subtly woven into the composition and my older brother identified for me the question-and-answer turn of the tune we know as "The Arkansas Traveller."

So, "The Arkansas Traveller" was a song, too.

And that was all I knew it to be until I was 22 years old.

Once I came back to Arkansas and entered the publishing endeavors therein, it did not take me long to realize that "The Arkansas Traveller" is perhaps the most significant component of Arkansas's folk legacy. But until a few months ago, I could not have recited it for you.

What *was* the tale? My curiosity compelled me to find out. My quest entailed much more research than I had anticipated. My eventual discovery, however, confirmed for me the degree of influence in our state's heritage with which the legend has been credited.

The legend of the Arkansas Traveller is essentially a skeleton dialogue which has been brought to life in countless forms. The dialogue has appeared in at least twelve printed versions and has inspired two paintings, several engravings, a lithograph and more than one dramatic production. *Kit, The Arkansas Traveler*, penned by Edward Spencer of Maryland and first performed in 1869 in Buffalo, New York, was, according to W. K. McNeil, "one of the staples of late Nineteenth-Century popular theatre." The Arkansas Traveler Theatre in Hardy, Arkansas, an outdoor ampitheatre built around an authentic log cabin, has since 1968 staged a skillful and sensitive production of the tale. Its "successful

8

summer-after-summer schedule" testifies to the appeal of the tale to native Arkansans and visitors alike.

Whether the tune or the tale came first is an oft-debated question. It is probably safe to assume that the tune existed prior to the legend, but that the legend has been responsible for its preservation. The tune, like the dialogue, has appeared in a variety of forms. An extensive chronicle of the treatment of the tune was written by W. K. McNeil and published in the October, 1981 issue of *The Arkansas Country Dancer*.

So why am I offering you yet another version? Surely the answer is obvious. Had it not been for a popular rock group, I might never have heard the tune of "The Arkansas Traveller." Had it not been for a trace of curiosity, I might never have known the tale. Even fewer stimuli are available to bring the legend to the attention of today's children than were available to me. The chances of an adolescent — or adult — Arkansan happening upon the tale have been dangerously diminished.

There is currently one book in print that includes any version of the tale at all; I refer to Sarah Fountain's anthology, *Arkansas Voices* (Little Rock: Rose Publishing Co., 1976). The evolution of the dialogue is given extensive treatment in James Masterson's *Tall Tales of Arkansaw* (Boston: Chapman and Grimes, 1942). Masterson devotes 34 pages to the legend, introducing and presenting all twelve versions of the dialogue, from the most familiar (that of Colonel Sandford C. Faulkner, whose version appeared in the mid-1800's) to the most ambitious (Fred Allsopp's poetic version, which consists of 130 rhymed couplets in trochaic tetrameter). *Tall Tales of Arkansaw* was reprinted in 1974 by Rose Publishing Company under the title *Arkansas Folklore*; unfortunately, both editions are now out of print.

I have chosen to present the legend in narrative form for several

9

reasons. It seemed likely that a narrative version would better lend itself to illustration than would the simple dialogue, and that illustration coupled with the story form might make the deepest impression on younger readers. The narrative supplement to the dialogue takes the reader beyond what is said to what is implied, to the motivations behind the speech.

I wish to stress that this adaptation is *not* the legend itself. It is but one of many expressions of the legend. One liberty I have taken is to set the story in the Ozark Mountains; the authorities tell us only that the encounter occurs in the Arkansas backwoods. Secondly, although none of the versions I have read takes the reader (or listener) any farther than the fiddler's invitation to the traveller to have supper and spend the night, I have extended their interaction. I took them through their supper and after-supper repose in order to shed a little more light on the personality of the fiddler. If this does not help you, I do not ask you to accept it. Rather, I would direct you to Masterson's work, from which you can draw your own conclusion about the characters and their relationship.

The Smith and Sadler children are grown now, and we are scattered across the United States from Texas to North Carolina. We ceased our summer camping trips five years ago. Our boat sat in our sideyard for several months, serving as both a reminder of our past and an invitation to perpetuate those good times. We talked occasionally of renovating the boat and renewing our ski trips, until there was little left to renovate. We talked, you see, as though the decay of our boat was keeping us from upholding our traditions. The truth is that the cessation of our traditions caused the boat's decay.

The material things that add pleasure to our lives — such as boats — are certain to disintegrate, either through disuse, abuse, overuse, or by their very organic nature. The intangible things that

add pleasure to our lives — such as folklore and music and literature — will decay under only one condition: Disuse.

I offer you this version of the legend of the Arkansas Traveller in order to keep it alive for yet another generation.

—Liz Smith Parkhurst
February, 1982

For Further Reading:

Hudgins, Mary D. "Arkansas Traveler — A Multi-Parented Wayfarer," *Arkansas Historical Quarterly*, vol. 9, no. 2 (Summer, 1971), pp. 145-160.

Masterson, James. "The Arkansas Traveler," *Arkansas Voices*, ed. Sarah Fountain. Little Rock, Rose Publishing Co., 1976, pp. 62-65.

Masterson, James. "A Traveler, A Cabin, and A Fiddle," *Arkansas Folklore*. Little Rock: Rose Publishing Co., 1974, pp. 186-254.

Masterson, James. "A Traveler, A Cabin, and A Fiddle," *Tall Tales of Arkansaw*. Boston: Chapman and Grimes, 1942, pp. 186-254.

McNeil, W. K. "Ozark Fiddle Tunes," *Arkansas Country Dancer*, vol. 2, no. 4 (October-December, 1981), pp.13-22.

The Arkansas Traveller

Have you ever been to the Ozark Mountains?

If you have, you know that nothing can greet you more heartily than an autumn sunrise in the Ozarks. The sunlight dances on the leaves of the blankets of trees, causing them to burst

into patches of gold, red and green, until the valley below you looks just like one of the brightly-colored quilts the mountain women are so famous for making.

You know, also, that as the sun climbs the horizon, the leaves begin to show off for you.

Releasing their grip on the powerful branches, they somersault through the air — tumbling, tumbling, tumbling, riding the wind until they land gracefully at your feet.

And you know the sound your feet make in the evening, when the sun begins its descent and the leaves no longer frolic but waltz solemnly in the twilight on the forest floor. You hear the crunch of the leaves under your feet . . . but that is only one of the sounds you hear in the Ozark evenings. The lower the sun sets, the more new sounds reach your ears. Perhaps that is because as long as there is light, you take in the wonders of the Ozarks with only your eyes, for the mountains offer an endless array of marvelous sights. Only when you can no longer see its wonders do you begin to listen to them.

If you are lucky enough to live there, or if you and your family are spending a vacation there, no doubt you will take your evening walk

along a modern paved road, and you will return to the place from which you began. In other words, you will have a shelter to return to, which you can call your own, if only for the night. Suppose, however, that you are only passing through, travelling alone by horseback, and that the dirt path you have been following all day is rapidly being covered by the very leaves that made you laugh earlier in the day. You look around you and you see only the outline of mountains; you look above you and you see only the moon, rising to relieve the sun of his day's work. It is one of those cloudy nights which do not lend you the light of the stars.

You are no longer seeing the Ozark Mountains: Now you are hearing them. Your day's journey is at an end. Now, tell me, where will you stay for the night?

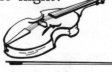

On a lusty autumn evening, a traveller guided his horse along a winding, dusty path. There wasn't going to be much path much longer, he was thinking to himself. Moment by moment, leaves were covering the forest floor while the sun sank below the silhouette of the mountains, pulling the blanket of dusk over the Ozark sky.

The traveller had come from the east and after one day of riding through the Ozark Mountains, he had noticed some quite remarkable things about the land. It was like no other mountain region he had ever seen (and this traveller had probably seen more of the United States than you or I have). It was an enchanting region, abundant in streams and creeks, peaks and valleys, jackrabbits and cardinals.

What the land seemed to lack was human population. He knew that beyond the Ozarks, there was a town called Little Rock (that was

where he was headed),but he had not encountered a single community during the entire day. He had spotted an occasional log cabin or dogtrot house, which was all the evidence he had that any people lived there at all.

What had impressed him most of all about the untamed Ozark Mountains was that it would simply not do to be lost there.

But night was falling, and he *was* lost!

The traveller pulled his horse to a stop and looked about him. He was in a valley, he surmised, because the tree-lined mountains towered above him on all sides. Above them a blue-gray sky was turning leisurely into a velvet purple.

As he peered into the twilight, the traveller heard a high-pitched melody, a tune which seemed to be asking a question. *I wonder what bird that is?* he mused. *I have never heard the likes of it before.* The melody sounded again.

And again. The traveller thrust his head forward and listened.

A fiddle. Our traveller knew the sound of a fiddle when he heard it. He played a fair tune himself when he got the chance. And if that was a fiddle — and what sounds like a fiddle that isn't a fiddle? — then there must be a human perched beneath it, unless the Ozark Mountains were even more unusual than he already thought them to be.

With a sigh of relief, he spurred his horse towards the persistent tune, the musical question. The trees soon parted into a clearing to reveal the silhouette of a log cabin. A faint gleam of lantern light above the doorway of the cabin drew him towards the first person he had seen all day and the first Ozark mountaineer he had seen in his life.

He was sitting on a barrel in the doorway of the cabin. The door itself stood open and ap-

peared to be made of an old bed frame covered with a bearskin. Next to the barrel lay a large mammal covered with glossy auburn fur. Only when it drowsily raised its head, having scented the stranger, was the traveller certain that it was a dog — of mixed breed, to be sure — and that it was in fact alive. The fiddler, who was apparently unaccustomed to shaving (and you'd think twice too, if it meant walking a quarter-mile for the water and putting a blade to your face without the benefit of a mirror), was playing the incomplete musical phrase over and over. Each time he reached the end, the last note seemed to freeze in the air, just as abruptly as the note in Musical Chairs which tells you to spring to action. But the fiddler did not spring to action each time he cut *his* melody short; he merely wrinkled his forehead, frowned and began the tune again. He really was not in a very good humour, between you and me. It did

not take the traveller long to discover this, either.

"Hello, kind sir," the traveller offered, realizing that his greeting had been persuaded by his hopeful thinking.

"Hallo, yoreself," the fiddler returned. If he looked up at all from his fiddle, it escaped the notice of the traveller. The dog issued an obligatory growl; having done his duty, he again lay his head between his front paws. But his ears remained erect and his tail rigid.

"How do you do?"

"I do pretty much as I please."

"I am very thirsty," the traveller ventured, still astride his horse. "Have you any spirits here?"

"You think my house is ha'nted?" The fiddler seemed to take offense. "If you want spirits, go look in the graveyard."

"You mistake my meaning. Have you any

liquor?"

"Had some yesterday, but my ole dog got in and lapped it all out of the pot."

"You don't understand; I don't mean pot liquor. I'm wet and cold and want some whiskey. Have you got any?"

"Yep," the fiddler replied, "in my stumick I do. Drunk our last drop this mornin'."

"Well, can you give me something to eat?"

"Ain't a durned thing in the house."

"Well, can you give my horse anything? He's earned *his* supper today."

The fiddler shrugged his shoulders. "Ain't earned it for *me*."

Well, as you can imagine, the traveller was beginning to get a little put out with the mountaineer. He knew that, as a rule, mountain folk had no reason to trust outsiders, so it would not help matters if he lost his temper. What was annoying him more than the fiddler's sassy

answers was that every time he finished a sentence, he would punctuate it with that tune — or rather, that half-tune.

The traveller began again. "I wouldn't be imposing on you so, my friend, except that I had expected to reach a town by sundown. Give me *some* satisfaction, if you please. Where does this road go to?"

"It's never gone nowhere since I been here."

"Well, then, how far is it to where it forks?"

"I ain't ever seen it fork, neither."

"And how long *have* you lived here?"

"D'ye see that mountain yonder? Well, it was here when I come here."

"Well," the traveller sighed, "it is dark and sure to rain again and, in spite of your generous directions, I'm not likely to get to any other house soon. Can't you let me sleep in yours? I'll tie my horse to a tree and we'll both do without food and drink."

"Sorry, stranger," the fiddler returned. "My house leaks. There's just one dry spot in it, and me and Sal sleeps there. You'd just as well sleep where you're sitting now."

"Why don't you finish covering your house and stop the leak?"

"'Cause it's been rainin' on and off all day."

"Then why don't you fix it when it's not raining?"

"'Cause it don't leak then!"

The traveller had just about run out of questions, but not out of determination to have a bed for the night. He realized by now that hospitality was something to be earned in the Ozarks. He paused to think, and his silence was accompanied by the sound of the fiddle.

Suddenly the traveller jerked his head up and demanded, "Why are you playing that tune over and over?"

"'Fraid I'll forget it" was the fiddler's

economic reply.

"And why don't you play the rest of it?" the traveller continued.

"'Cause *it* I already forgot!"

The traveller fixed his eyes on the fiddler and said, in a low but intense voice, "Do you mind if I try?"

The fiddler met the traveller's gaze for the first time. "Stranger," he finally said, "can you play the fiddle?"

"Oh, a little," the traveller teased. "When I have the chance."

"You don't *look* it," the fiddler mused, "but if you think you can play any more onto that tune, I reckon you can try. Don't move — I'll

32

bring the fiddle to you. I don't want you in here."

The fiddler handed his instrument and bow to the traveller, who remained astride his horse. The traveller slowly lifted the fiddle to his left shoulder and poised the bow above it. With the care and precision of a woodcarver making a toy for his grandson, he played the phrase he

had heard a hundred times in the past half-hour. Pausing long enough to wink at the mountaineer, mounted on his barrel, the traveller completed the tune with the grace and rhythm of a doe clearing a fence.

For a moment the mountaineer said nothing. Then he lifted his eyes and directed the traveller, in even and uncommitting syllables, "Play it again."

Which the traveller did.

Before the traveller could lower the instrument to his lap, the mountaineer had bounced off the barrel like a marionette, flung himself around in the doorway and begun to bellow to his wife and children whom, until now, the traveller had neither seen nor heard.

"Sal, stir yoreself round like a six-horse team in a mud hole and cook up some of that buck I kilt this mornin' in the holler! Dick, feed

this gentleman's horse and take it under the shed! Lizzie! Spread out some beddin' for this here guest of ourn!"

A boy of about twelve years and a girl some four years younger burst forth from the house in response to their father's call. Upon

seeing the gallant figure upon his steed, they stopped short. Once they had taken in his city dress to their full satisfaction, they leaped forward again and practically pulled him off his horse to exhibit their hospitality. They then skipped away to perform their respective tasks.

37

The dog, with considerably less agility, pulled himself to his feet and followed Dick to the stable, slowly wagging his tail.

Reaching into the doorway of his cabin, the fiddler produced a large, earthen jug and offered it to his guest. "Stranger, draw on this jug o' whiskey 'til Sal has our supper ready. And for land's sakes, git in this ole house where sits a fire!"

An hour later, the traveller was pushing his chair back from the head of the knotty pine table. He had just finished the tenderest deer meat and warmest cornbread one could want on a drafty, damp Ozark night. His host invited him to draw his chair up to the fireplace. The host had already picked up his fiddle again and was now playing the tune — the *entire* tune — over again. He wasn't going to forget it *this* time.

The traveller took his seat by the fire, and

the children and dog placed themselves
wordlessly at his feet, as if they expected him to
perform a magical trick. As the host played his
fiddle, the traveller reached into the pocket of
his waistcoat and drew out a beautifully-
molded, long-stemmed clay pipe and a pouch of

sweet-smelling tobacco. "Do you smoke?" he asked the fiddler, as he methodically filled his pipe with tobacco.

The fiddler looked up from his musical task and grinned. "When I git the chance," he replied.

"Ah, I forget that tobacco is not grown around these parts," the traveller said. "You have a pipe, though?"

The fiddler put his instrument aside and reached onto the mantelpiece. With great pride, he showed his trusty corncob pipe to his guest. "Don't git to use it much," he said, "so it still works like new!"

"Tell me if you like the taste of this tobacco," the traveller said, dividing his tobacco between the clay pipe and the corncob pipe. "If you do, I will leave you a good supply of it. I should be happy to make it a present to you, to show my thanks for your hospitality."

The fiddler drew on his pipe for a few minutes. "That is some fine pipe tobacky, friend, and I couldn't turn down an offer like that. But just for the record, I owe *you* one now." He picked up his fiddle. "You give *me* a present afore you come in."

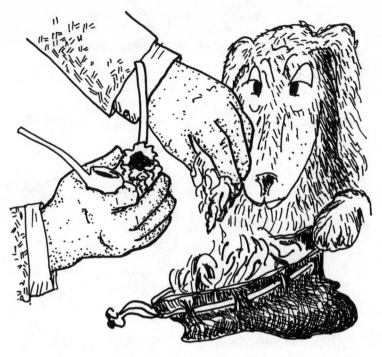

Again the fiddler played his newly-discovered jig. The finality with which he delivered his last note made it clear that his performance for the night was over. A simple twist of his eyebrows made it equally clear to Dick and Lizzie that their bedtime had arrived. The reluctance with which they rose to their feet was only exceeded by that of their dog.

Dick solemnly extended his right hand to his guest. While they exchanged a firm and most genteel handshake, Lizzie shyly kissed the traveller's cheek. Their old dog, now on his feet, wagged his tail for a moment — then the three of them retired to their beds.